SERIES EDITOR: LEE JOHNSC

OSPREY NEW VANGUARD SE

MERKAVA
MKs I, II & III
CHARIOT OF STEEL

TEXT BY
SAMUEL M. KATZ

COLOUR PLATES BY
PETER SARSON

ISBN 1 85532 643 4

Filmset in Great Britain
Printed through Worldprint Ltd, Hong Kong

Military Editor Iain MacGregor
Designed by the Black Spot

For a catalogue of all books published by Osprey Military please write to:
The Marketing Manager, Osprey Publishing Ltd,
Michelin House, 81 Fulham Road, London SW3 6RB

Artist's Note

Readers may care to note the original paintings from which the colour plates in this book were prepared are available for private sale. All reproduction copyright whatsoever is retained by the publisher. All enquiries should be addressed to:

Peter Sarson, 46 Robert-Louis Stevenson Avenue, Westbourne Bournemouth, Dorset BH4 8EJ

The publishers regret that they can enter into no correspondence upon this matter.

Editor's note

Due to Israeli security constraints placed upon the author, information on the internal workings of this vehicle has resulted in a limited number of annotations available for the cutaway featured, and, on certain plates and photographs the identity of the units has been withheld. Also, all information within the book regarding the 211th Armored Brigade has been taken from previously published accounts.

Readers may wish to read this title in conjunction with the following Osprey titles:

New Vanguard 2 *M1 Abrams*
New Vanguard 3 *Sherman*
New Vanguard 6 *T-72*
New Vanguard 7 *IS-2*
New Vanguard 12 *BMP*
Elite 8 *Israeli Defense Forces Since 1973*
Elite 18 *Israeli Elite Units Since 1948*
Elite 45 *Armies of the Gulf War*
MAA 127 *Israeli Army in the Middle East Wars 1948-73*
MAA 165 *Armies in Lebanon 1982-84*
MAA 194 *Arab Armies of the Middle East Wars 1948-73*

MERKAVA MBT
MKs I, II & III

INTRODUCTION

Scanning through his field glasses on a barren training field somewhere in Israel's north, a young lieutenant, a Merkava Mk III commander, stands in his turret as his powerful vehicle grinds a path on the cold, hard volcanic ground. A target appears 1,900 metres away and must be obliterated, preferably on the first shot. Hopping back inside the tank, in order to stand on his commanders chair, the young 'Ma'Tak' (Hebrew acronym for tank commander) orders the turret swung 40° to the right, the gun placed at a minus 3° trajectory, and an APFSDS round loaded into the breech of the tank's 120mm main armament cannon. 'Steady,' the lieutenant utters into his communications gear, 'let's place this round dead-centre on the cross-hairs.' Three seconds pass and finally the order 'Esh' (fire) is issued. A thunderous blast emanates from the hulking armoured beast, cracking through the mountainous landscape with resonating power. A thick cloud of smoke and dust engulfs the tank, but the gunner monitors the round through his high-optic sights. In the valley below, what was once a Syrian Army BTR-60 armoured personnel carrier receives the Merkava's offering near the driver's compartment. The APFSDS round cuts through the armoured vehicle like a red-hot knife through butter, and causes it to erupt in a shattering ball of flames and debris.

'Excellent' boasts the tank commander to his crew. 'Come back to earth, lieutenant,' barks the battalion CO, listening in on the communications net. 'With this tank I expect nothing less than excellence.'

For the remainder of the morning, nearly a dozen Merkava Mk IIIs will, courtesy of their 120mm main armament cannons, fill the Golan Heights with the volcanic serenade of tank fire. The Israeli Defense Force (IDF) has invested a lot of money in simulators to teach its crews how to place a round square dead centre into the weak spot of an enemy tank, but no computerised contraption could ever replace the electric atmosphere of the interaction inside the turret, the tugging of the Nomex coveralls and the pull of the Kevlar helmet. No Sega-like gizmo could ever reproduce the bark of the tank commander, standing upright and clutching his microphone, as the dry mud caked on his boot disintegrates all over the fire-control systems and the laser range-

Before there was a 'Chariot' there was the concept, the design and a wooden mock-up just to determine if all the blueprints, sketches and plastic models looked quite the same with a life-size model. Here, the first wooden mock-up of the first Merkava design is on display at the IDF Museum in Tel Aviv. (Samuel M. Katz)

finder. Of course, nothing could ever hope to replicate the blast of the cannon's roar and the choking sensation of cordite entering one's nostrils and lungs. That is what such exercises are meant to accomplish. Simulators can hone certain skills. Only manoeuvres can prepare the soldier for war.

War is what these Merkava Mk IIIs were designed to deter and, inescapably, fight. The Mk III, as the Barak Brigade tankers demonstrate this blisteringly cold morning, are machines of fire and steel produced and forged with the purpose of destroying an enemy who is also equipped with the machines, intent and training to reciprocate in kind. The modern battlefield is one congested with smart weapons and missiles that can eat through armour like a chainsaw through dry-rot. Tank cannons, now nearly the size of battleship guns, are mounted on tanks with computerised systems that make hitting a target, even in darkness, fog, or a thick cloud of burning metal and blood, a simple proposition. Their ordnance, nasty little devils that can spin through armour in seconds and obliterate the insides of a turret, fly faster and explode larger than at any time before. In the end, when a tank battle has ended, it is the one standing up (or not on fire) that declares victory.

A side view of the initial Merkava design and wooden mock-up. Note the rather rectangular turret of this first edition; a very different turret would eventually be produced for the first tanks introduced into service in the late 1970s. (Samuel M. Katz)

The first Merkava rolled off production and presented to the 7th Armored Brigade commander, Col. Avigdor Kahalani – the first-ever Israeli-produced MBT. Note how the sloped turret differs markedly from the Centurion (parked to its left), and how unique hull design was meant to provide enemy ordnance with few hard angles to penetrate. The photograph shows to advantage the Merkava's unique and revolutionary wedge-shaped turret design. (Samuel M. Katz)

With seven major wars behind it and more inevitably in the path, the State of Israel is pinning its hopes on the Merkava as the type of tank that will be left standing. Although it is a tank that is relatively new to the world of Main Battle Tanks (MBTs), it has travelled a long and arduous road of nearly 50 years.

BACKGROUND

The Merkava has, indeed, travelled a long route from inception to the nation's first line of defence against the Syrian Army, and it has survived an often bumpy road. The decision to produce an indigenous Israeli main battle tank dates back to the 1956 War, when, for the first time in Israeli military history, the tank proved to be the decisive weapon fielded in battle. The 1948 War was an infantry campaign with little armour, and the subsequent counter-guerrilla operations of the early 1950s involved special forces and irregular warfare. Israeli armour in 1956 consisted of ageing World War Two-era Shermans, French-built AMX-13 light tanks, and any other armoured bits that could be found on the scrap heaps of Europe. Tank warfare, as the battles of the Second World War indicated, was the dominant form of land warfare and, as a result, likely to be the factor deciding a major Arab-Israeli conflagration in the

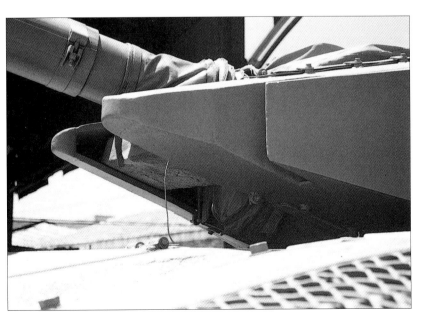

Final touches are applied to a Merkava Mk I at one of the main production facilities in central Israel. The photograph shows the support structure for the wheels and suspension system, as well as the add-on rear-turret storage bin basket, now a part of all Merkava models. (IGPO)

future. In 1956, a primitive struggle by today's standards, Israel was already outgunned by Soviet-built tanks fielded by Egypt; Egyptian T-34s were faster and better equipped for the travails of desert warfare than the Shermans, and the ISIII Stalin tanks were armoured like nothing else on the battlefield. Following the war, however, the Egyptians replaced their ageing Soviet-built World War Two-era tanks with T-54s – Israel needed to obtain modern, heavy tanks, and fast.

Early IDF armour

In 1960, the Israeli government and Great Britain reached an agreement on the purchase of nearly 50 Centurion MBTs. Nicknamed *Sho'* ('Whip') by the IDF, they were the first modern tanks to be deployed by the Israelis and at the time were the most modern piece of hardware in the Middle East. In early 1964, the Israeli government arranged for several of its officers to travel to Germany and undergo a secret training course in the operation of the American-made M48 Patton. Both the Centurion and M48 were virtually obsolete the moment they were painted in Israeli colours, but they were far more suitable for full-scale warfare than the M50 Shermans and AMX-13 tanks then in front line service with IDF tank units. They were certainly more worthy opponents to the T-34s and T-54/T-55s flying the Egyptian, Syrian and Iraqi flags. By having Centurions and Pattons in its order of battle, the IDF also had to reach tactical parody with Jordan, whose British-trained, highly disciplined and motivated army also operated both the Centurion and Patton, and posed a strategic threat to the east. But in 1964 the IDF was small and primitive by today's standards, and although it was an army with some very serious problems, there were some very innovative ideas to solve them.

Israeli generals, all veterans of the brutal 1948 War of Independence where armour played virtually no role because Israel possessed only a handful of tanks, realised that the next full-scale conflagration between Israel and her Arab neighbours would be a tank war. There would be bloody, large-scale tank battles of the type not seen on the battlefield since the Second World War. Many Israeli officers had learned in their courses in the United States, Great Britain and France, that full-scale tank warfare meant heavy casualties. Tanks got hit, suffered mechanical failures, and vehicles and crews needed to be replaced. In a tank battle, many believed, an attrition rate above 50 per cent for vehicles was not uncommon. Israeli generals realised that in order for Israel to win a full-scale war, it would need a sizeable fleet of tanks, top-quality MBTs, that were suited to Israel's specific geographic and tactical requirements. Many generals and Ministry of Defense officials dreamt of Israel producing its own vehicle, but these visionaries were restrained only by the boundaries of their imagination. In fact, the huge differences between their ideas and the money and resources available meant that Ministry of Defense planners still needed to live within the bounds of reality. In 1965 and 1966, reality meant the United Kingdom.

The 'Six Day' War

In October 1966, two Chieftain MBTs arrived in Israel in great secrecy for extensive trials with the IDF Armored Corps; British engineers, also operating in Israel under considerable secrecy, supervised the project. The British offered the IDF a deal for the joint co-operation venture. The British needed money in order to complete the development of the 'Chieftain', a modern tank with a 120mm cal. main armament gun; and the Israelis needed tanks. Israel agreed to purchase hundreds of old Centurions at a significant discount in exchange for the opportunity of being allowed to take part in the final stages of the Chieftain tank's development. Britain would sell the IDF Chieftains and help build an assembly line in Israel to manufacture an indigenous version of the tank, under licence. At first treated with tremendous resolve and vigour, the relationship crumbled when the first shots were fired initiating the 1967 Six Day War between Israel and Egypt, Jordan, Syria and Iraq.

While the fight against Jordan and Syria in 1967 was primarily an infantry campaign, the Israeli juggernaut in Sinai was a tank blitz. The Centurions and Pattons of the 7th Armored Brigade had cut through the most daunting of Egyptian defences and had proved to themselves and

Days before the Israeli military launched its invasion of Lebanon in June 1982, tanks from Eli Geva's armored brigade, designated in published accounts as the 211th, line up for inspection – the engine compartment hood is open for the unit's chief mechanical officer to inspect. Many military observers scoffed at the notion of a forward-positioned engine, but their 'expert' observations were proved wrong during the Lebanon conflict. (IDF Spokesman)

their Egyptian foes that an unrelenting armoured force, trained to hit targets at ranges up to 2,000 metres, was unbeatable on the battlefield. As one-sided as the Israeli victory was, most of the Israeli casualties from 1967 were those who wore the black beret and *Heyl Ha'Shirion* beret badge of the Armored Corps. Of the 600 dead in 1967, nearly one tenth came from the 7th Armored Brigade alone, and many more were seriously wounded. Dozens of tanks had been hit and destroyed by Egyptian tank, anti-tank and small-arms fire, and the toll on Israel's armoured stock was considerable. Egyptian tank gunners had scored considerable success with their 85mm and 100mm main armament cannons, and although the large picture vindicated Israel's strategic deployment of armour, the attrition of tanks and manpower on the brigade, battalion and company level was such that the victory was not an all-encompassing one. There was still room for improvement even in the glory of the Israeli victory.

Britain pulls out of arms treaty

As the Israeli flag was hoisted over territories seized in the conflict, the Armored Corps' joint venture with the British came to an abrupt end. Following the war, just as Israel's need for a sudden infusion of tanks into its order of battle became acute, the UK cancelled the project, bowing to political pressure from the Arabs. A military relationship of long-term significance had been snuffed by the fickleness of politics. It was a lesson with long term implications that the Israeli Ministry of Defense, to this day, does not forget or forgive and was the driving force behind Israel's determination not to search elsewhere for her next generation of MBT.

In 1967 Israel reacted the only way it could, by refusing to supply the

'Go ahead, make my day!' A 7th Armored Brigade Merkava Mk I assumes a forward line firing position somewhere on the Golan Heights. Better than any analytical description of design and performance, the photograph ideally illustrates what it was that the Merkava was designed to do – defend territory by being almost unhittable on an open battlefield. (IDF Spokesman)

British with its recommendations for modifications to the Chieftain, feedback that the British Ministry of Defence and the manufacturers of the Chieftain desperately wanted. According to reports, the British informed Maj.-Gen. Tal and his development staff of their final decision a year after they had acquiesced to the Arab demands so that Israeli feedback in the Chieftain's design could be analysed and incorporated into the final variant. The British Ministry of Defence had also lobbied the United States Department of Defense, persuading them not to sell the IDF any American tanks, so that the Israelis would be forced to follow through with the now doomed Chieftain project.

This game of revenge and counter-strike set back the Israeli programme by a generation. Most worrisome for the IDF was the British decision to cancel the exchange just as Egypt and Syria took delivery of their first Soviet-produced T-62 tanks, then the top-of-the-line MBT in the Warsaw Pact order of battle. It was 1969 and Israel was embroiled in fighting the multi-front War Of Attrition against the conventional armies of Egypt, Jordan and Syria, as well as Palestinian guerrillas. Israel still had no new tank of its own, as one by one, cargo ships arriving from the Soviet Union unloaded their cargoes of brand new T-62s into the ports of Alexandria and Latakia.

Birth of the Merkava project

In August 1970, after a budgetary battle with Defense Minister Moshe Dayan, a man who wanted nothing to do with the project, the Finance Minister gave a thumb's up to the indigenous programme. At the time, the Armored Corps had five options in military and financial terms concerning the next generation Israeli main battle tank. They could obtain

Israel-Syrian border, winter 1981. In a unique picture, not at all characteristic of the conception of the Israeli geography as a land surrounded by desert, a 7th Armored Brigade Merkava Mk I patrols part of Mount Hermon, covered by nearly ten feet of snow. (Israeli MOD)

An impressive ring of steel at a forward encampment for a Merkava battalion near the Lebanese border in June 1982. The fact that what were then new rear-turret storage bins have been affixed to the turret (and are crammed with the crew's sleeping kit, extra ammo and supplies, etc.) indicates that this tank unit is ready for a long-term cross-border deployment. Israeli tank crews like to carry everything with them to battle, from radio boom-boxes to additional sleeping bags for comfort; note how a stretcher has been affixed to the rear area of the lead Merkava. (IDF Spokesman)

large numbers of the ageing M48 Patton, overhaul their engines and rearm their turrets with the 105mm cannon at a cost of 724,000 Israeli Lira per tank; they could refit the Pattons with new engines, a modified turret-housing to accommodate an experimental 110mm main armament cannon, and install an advanced NBC warfare system; they could purchase large numbers of American-produced M60 Pattons at a cost of 822,000 Israeli Lira per tank; they could acquiesce to British demands and purchase the Chieftain at a cost of 1,188,000 Lira per tank; or finally, they could design, develop and produce an indigenous tank built specifically to Israeli standards, the Merkava, at a cost of 906,000 Israeli Lira per tank. The initial number of tanks to be purchased, modified or produced in this programme was approximately 300. There was only one man, Defense Ministry officials knew, able to lead the project. That man was Maj.-Gen. Yisrael 'Talik' Tal.

Father of the Chariot

Born in 1924 in Be'er Tuvia, near Tiberias in Galilee, Tal volunteered into the British Army in 1942; he served in the 2nd Battalion of the Jewish Brigade and saw action in northern Italy against German forces. As much of the 'Jewish' element of the British Army returned to Palestine following V-E day, Tal remained in Italy along with fellow *Haganah* personnel to participate in getting the massive *Rechesh* (acquisition) programme under way. It is here, many believe, where Tal's penchant for quality control and inspection was born, but he was considered a natural at evaluating equipment, no matter how old and decrepit, and devising ways to reinstate that very equipment into top-grade serviceable condition. An infantry officer for a good part of his career, with a reputation as a disciplinarian, Tal was appointed the deputy commander of the Armored Branch. From 1960 to 1964 he commanded the 7th Armored Brigade and forged foreign contacts to solidify the IDF's acquisition of a modern armoured fighting vehicle. For

A Mk I demonstrates its ability to race at speeds of about 40mph as it responds to a forward firing area during manoeuvres on the Golan Heights. Note the driver's head, visible through the dust and debris, and the tank commander standing upright in his turret perch, fingers never far away from the trigger of his commander's FN MAG 7.62mm light machine gun. (IDF Spokesman)

the brigade during 'Talik's' tenure, it was the age of the Centurion – at that point the most modern piece of equipment to be found anywhere in the Middle East. When he handed over the reins of the brigade to Col. Shmuel 'Gorodish' Gonen in 1964, it was 'Talik's' insistence that led to the first stages of the Patton programme.

Because 'Talik' had been in uniform since pre-independence days, he was acutely aware of the difficulties Israel faced in arms procurement and the dangers that this presented during times of war. Israel had possessed an indigenous arms-producing industry even before its independence; the *Haganah*, the pre-independence underground, had built its own guns and ammunition since 1929. Producing 9mm ammu-

An excellent close-up view of the driver's position in the Merkava Mk. I, and the means by which chassis and turret meet. The photograph also shows the drivers reinforced periscope. (IDF Spokesman)

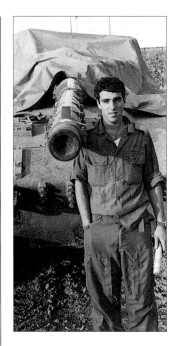

A young 188th Barak Brigade tank commander poses for the camera alongside the 'business end' of his tank's most lethal component at a forward bivouac area in southern Lebanon. Note close-up view of thermal sleeve for the M68 gun, as well as of the gun's muzzle reference sensor. (IDF Spokesman)

nition was one thing, as was mass-producing a relatively simple weapon like the *Uzi*, but building and mass-producing a 60-ton tank, one with sophisticated range-finding gear and armour protection was a daunting challenge. Yet even before the end of the Chieftain deal, Maj.-Gen. Yisrael 'Talik' Tal, a tank officer whose philosophy of quick and lightning attack was the armoured thesis behind the victory of the 1967 Six Day War, was the man who lobbied for the production of an Israeli-built tank and the man who inherited the job of supervising the tank's design, development and production. In the eyes of the Armored Corps, there was tremendous urgency in getting this indigenous programme off the ground; as allies and weapons suppliers, the British and French were notoriously fickle and unreliable. Israeli fears were justified in both aspects of the Anglo-French deal. Following the 1967 War, the French embargoed all arms sales to Israel, including Sa'ar missile boats and Mirage jets which had already been paid for.

THE CHARIOT PROGRAMME

With nearly US $100 million of funding from the usually cash-strapped Ministry of Defense invested into the development and production of the Merkava programme, work on the indigenous Israeli tank began in 1971. 'Talik's' objective in designing and developing the 'Israeli tank' were three-fold: to provide the IDF with its first ever state-of-the-art main battle tank (in its history, no country had ever agreed to sell the IDF a new tank); to guarantee that a foreign-led arms embargo could never deny the IDF a continuous supply of tanks; and, that the indigenous designed main battle tank be built to Israeli specifications, to meet the unique needs of the IDF (the new tank was not intended to be an off-the-shelf type item for mass export).

Tal hand-picked some of Israel's most capable engineers and tank officers to participate in the project, known as '*Tochnit Ha'Merkava*' ('Chariot Programme'). The tank had to be revolutionary but frugal, cost-efficient though powerful, made from home-produced material and technology, but able to meet and overcome the most modern Soviet

A modified Mk I on the move on the Golan Heights indicates the actual light weight of the ball and chain system, as its swishes and sways with the movement of the tank. Note also the Mk I's external 60mm mortar, mounted near the commander's cupola on the side of the turret. (IDF Spokesman)

built tanks encountered in the Arab arsenals. The question then, was not whether or not it was justifiable to develop and manufacture a tank in Israel, but whether it was within Israel's limited capability to carry out such an ambitious plan, both from the technological and industrial points of view. In addition, there was the question of whether it was possible in terms of price, and without hurting the economy in Israel. Some argued that Israel should continue to acquire existing main battle tanks, such as the Centurion and Patton, and completely re-fit them with Israeli-produced electronics, hydraulics, mechanics, and other additions that Israel's lessons on the battlefield had taught. But initial studies showed that applying developing systems to existing tanks was not only expensive, but still result, in the IDF fielding an antiquated system with modern technology. It was a stop-gap approach, not a plan for the future. 'Talik' would have none of it. Israel needed independent armour.

The 'Yom Kippur' War, 1973

By 1973, the IDF had gone from being a conscript army with only one conscript tank brigade, the 7th, to a multi-divisional fighting force fielding nearly a dozen tank brigades staffed by conscripts, with well over a dozen additional brigades manned by reservists. These civilian-soldiers served in formations ranging from Centurion units, to those fielding ageing Shermans (and even captured T-54/T-55s). Under Maj.-Gen. Tal's leadership as Chief Armor Officer from 1964 to 1969, the IDF had slowly developed into one of the most capable tank armies anywhere in the world. Israeli tank training was legendary: from Fort Knox to Salisbury Plain, Israeli tank gunning skills were considered to be the best in the world, and with the IAF acting as aerial artillery, *Heyl Ha'Shirion*'s armour legions were blessed with the most capable close-air support in the region. When the Egyptian and Syrian armies launched their brilliant surprise attack against Israeli positions along the Suez Canal and the Golan Heights on 6 October 1973 at 14:10 hours, Israel's iron shield came crashing down. From the sands of Sinai to the Valley of Tears, Israeli tanks found themselves outnumbered, heavily outma-

noeuvred, and fighting with dwindling firepower and reserves. Using Soviet doctrine, the Egyptian and Syrian armies were able to move large formations of T-62s and T-55s and seize ground with the support of infantry, many of whom were equipped with hand-held anti-tank weapons such as the RPG-7 and the AT-3 Sagger. Israeli armour doctrine, dictating that engagements should be fought at ranges of 2,000 metres, was shattered. On the Golan Heights, an entire Centurion Brigade, the 188th *Barak* (Lightning) was destroyed, while the 7th Brigade in the northern sector of the heights was fighting a close-quarter mÍlée at ranges as close as five metres. The mighty Centurion had proved itself highly vulnerable. So had the M48 and the M60. On top of the Golan Heights, the casualties were intense, but the tank combat was close-range and brutal. In Sinai, where the distances were greater, the armour casualties were just as high. The skills of the Arab tank crews had increased, as had the equipment in their arsenal and the ammunition they fired. The Israeli tanks were still better than the Soviet-built vehicles in the Arab arsenals, but large numbers of tanks were hit and many destroyed. Israel had won its epic armour engagements, but this was due primarily to the incredible tenacity of brigade and battalion commanders, and the impregnable courage of the tank crews. Still, as many Israeli generals knew, courage was not a thesis on which to base an armoured doctrine for an increasingly congested and technologically dominated battlefield.

Over 6,000 tanks – Arab and Israeli – participated in the 1973 War, and over 2,500 Israeli soldiers were killed in the conflict; the great majority of them were tank soldiers whose epic stands amid the advancing enemy armour saved the nation from probable destruction. Yet Israel is not a nation which could afford such rampant loss of life in battle. Not only is every casualty mourned as a national loss, but the loss of so many experienced tank soldiers, most of them veteran reservists, seriously weakened the strength of *Heyl Ha'Shirion* (the IDF Armored Corps) for the next, inevitable conflict. In economic terms, the destruction of so many tanks by enemy fire was a supreme burden on a nation whose national budget was already overwhelmed by defence expenditure. The attrition of hundreds of tanks in a prolonged conventional was limited by Israel's strategic depth in war. These armoured fighting machines were not custom ordered models built to Israeli combat specifications, but off-the-shelf surplus. Exacerbating the situation was the fact that all these tanks were produced abroad; their resupply was dependent on the ability and the political desire of a foreign nation to meet Israel's defence needs. For a nation's defence, it was an intolerable situation and one which demanded a solution.

The 1973 War devastated the Israel Defense Forces and the Armored Corps far more than any other of the IDF's six combat branches; nearly 1,500 of the IDF's 2,500 dead had been tank soldiers. With so many of its commanding officers dead and wounded, and so many tanks destroyed and damaged, top IDF commanders wondered whether the corps could recover from the 'October Earthquake'. Given the precarious situation on the frontiers, *Heyl Ha'Shirion* was not afforded the opportunity to regroup and quietly rebuild; it was still at war. There was no easy Israeli military victory in 1973. The shock of the surprise attack with its initial setbacks demoralised the IDF, as well as the Israeli nation as a whole. Instead of returning home to jubilant crowds celebrating another sweeping victory, the men of the IDF found themselves remaining at the front, engaged in a vicious and continuing war of attrition. The tanks lost by Egypt and Syria during the 18 days of fighting had been replaced immediately by their Soviet allies in a massive arms resupply effort. Israel received quite generous emergency arms supplies from the United States as well, but with almost all of its combat personnel at the front, *Heyl Ha'Shirion*'s task of absorbing the new tanks and armoured vehicles was an onerous one.

Rebuilding the Armored Corp

The task of rebuilding and rehabilitating the Armored Corps was led by Maj.-Gen. Moshe 'Musa' Peled, who became the IDF Armored Corps'

Another lesson learned in Lebanon concerning the proliferation of anti-tank mines resulted in this unique Israeli-produced device–the Mine Clearing Roller System (MCRS) produced by Netzer Sereni Metal Works and Urdan Industries, Ltd. The rollers were able to defeat the strongest of anti-tank land mines without damaging the tank or harming its crew. (IDF Spokesman)

ninth commander on 16 April 1974. 'Musa' faced enormous problems. Although the borders were now quiet, and a more relaxed defensive posture was possible, the Armored Corps still had to be rebuilt from scratch. But the lessons learned in 1973 were heeded, and most tanks and APCs were upgraded in armour protection to minimise crew casualties. The MBT upgrading took many shapes and forms, some quite basic, others ingenious. To increase protection against infantry anti-tank weapons, additional .30 and .50 cal. machine guns were placed on the tanks. To decrease damage from anti-tank weapons such as the RPG and Sagger, add-on armour plating was introduced to the Centurion and M60. Known as 'Blazer' reactive armour, these armour plates were meant to explode on impact, severely limiting the penetrative ability of armour-piercing projectiles. Although these additions increased vehicle weight and decreased mobility, it was felt that crew safety was paramount and that was exactly what Tal and his team were working on.

Four years after the Armored Corps endured its most serious test of survival, Maj.-Gen. Tal confirmed what had been rumoured for years: Israel was, indeed, working on an indigenous main battle tank. Details would not be released about this mysterious 50-ton plus war machine, but Tal promised that it would be both revolutionary and exceptional. The tank's delivery date was scheduled for the spring of 1979. Everyone at the programme was hoping that the schedule would and could be met. They hoped that war wouldn't break out in the interim.

On 11 March 1978, a Palestinian suicide squad launched from southern Lebanon landed on Israel's Mediterranean coast half-way between Tel Aviv and Haifa and seized two bus-loads of holiday travellers. In the ensuing stand-off with security forces near a vital Tel Aviv junction, 38 hostages were killed and 70 wounded in one of the worst terrorist outrages ever perpetrated inside the Jewish State. On 13 March 1978, the IDF, with the Armored Corps in the vanguard, entered southern Lebanon to root out the PLO terrorist presence from Israel's vulnerable

...s the Mk I's line of production ...ame to an end, and the Mk II ...as planned, designed and ...nder production, many Mk Is ...ere modified with Mk II tech-...ology. Here, a Mk I on the Golan ...eights is equipped with ...odified side-skirt armour par-...cular to the Mk II tank. (Israeli ...OD)

northern frontier. The small-scale military involvement in southern Lebanon, a harbinger of worse to come, proved to many in the IDF General Staff that war did not have to be limited to the ideal geographic killing grounds of Sinai or the Golan plateau. War involving large numbers of Israeli forces could be fought in urban areas amid a large civilian population. This would be the type of terrain that would find the tank vulnerable and exposed to the lethal anti-tank ordnance carried by guerrillas and terrorists. The project to design a MBT, one built specifically to Israel's requirements, took on an added sense of urgency.

Main aims for the Chariot programme

In heading the Merkava project, 'Talik' was adamant that any Israeli design would have the crew's personal protection as a paramount objective; the vehicle would have to be capable of withstanding an enormous amount of punishment without endangering the crew's lives. Since crew protection was the over-riding concern, every aspect of the tank had to adapt to this demand; firepower would have to come second and mobility, third. In addition, the tank would have to be large enough, and sufficiently comfortable, to accommodate a four-man crew through long hours of operational duty, and eventually, combat. With Israel's limited resources restricting the number of vehicles which could be produced, the tank would have to be the best in the world.

The Merkava project, intensified at the same time as Israel's production of its own indigenous fighter-bomber aircraft, the *Kfir* (or 'Lion Cub'). This had begun in 1968 after the French embargoed Mirage V fighter bombers already paid for by Israel. A short while later, the Israelis received the plans for the aircraft from a Swiss aircraft designer found by *Mossad* who was sympathetic to Israel's plight.

Protection, manoeuvrability and weaponry

Maj.-Gen. Tal had been the IDF's deputy Chief of Staff during the 1973 War and it angered him that so many tank soldiers had died in the conflict because the IDF was not fielding as modern and uniquely suited a tank as possible. He used the bitter conflict as a post-mortem laboratory to determine the cause for such heavy tank casualties in the Israeli ranks and to find remedies to incorporate in the planned Israeli-produced MBT to prevent such loss in future conflicts. Through exhaustive examinations of ballistic findings, Tal and his team of tank battle experts were able to produce a working idea of what the Israeli super tank had to be like. The primary concept was to make every part of the tank play its part in the crew's protection; it became known as 'spaced-armour'. Every physical aspect of the MBT, from fuel, ammunition and tools, performed a distinctive defensive function. The spacious interior would also incorporate the driver in the crew's compartment, removing a long-time tank crewman's psychological stigma.

The differences between the Mk I and Mk II are clearly seen in this photograph – the add-on armour plates around the turret, and the improved attachment loops for the side-skirt armour. (Israeli MoD)

Tal travelled to friendly Western nations to view the latest advances in the tank designs of the late 1970s; he witnessed prototypes of the West German Leopard, the French AMX-30, an advanced look, in Britain, of the new Chieftain and of the American XM-1. According to foreign reports, Israeli intelligence connections in eastern Europe had afforded 'Talik' a glimpse of the Soviet T-72 long before they were engaged on the battlefield of Lebanon.

Maj.-Gen. Tal was impressed by the Western tanks – and even by the latest Soviet offerings. But the Israeli landscape was far removed from the flat fields of Germany where a NATO-Warsaw Pact conflagration was expected. The Merkava needed to be suited to rough terrain, given the mountains to the north of Israel, and desert hills in the east; as the peace treaty was still a dream, the tank would also have to be a superb desert warrior. At first a wooden mock-up of the Merkava was produced and, later, various arms-producing firms in Israel were recruited to manu-

One of the first production series of Mk IIs rolls off the assembly line in central Israel in 1983. Unveiled with little fanfare and pressed into immediate front-line service in southern Lebanon, the Mk II was considered a marked improvement (in terms of armour and electronics) over the Mk I. (Israeli MOD)

facture the fire-control systems, special armour plating casting, shock absorbers and sights needed for the IDF's next generation of MBT. Speed was not an important factor, but size and security were.

A behemoth of an MBT, the Merkava proved a truly unique design with the turret and fighting compartment situated at the rear of the tank; the engine was placed up front, providing the crew with additional armoured protection. Because of the experience of IDF tank units in 1967 and particularly in the 1973 War, it was crucial to Maj.-Gen. Tal that the new tank be user-friendly in terms of maintenance. Tanks suffering minor hits on the Golan Heights during the 1973 War, for example, were often out of action for up to 24 hours while engines were replaced. The Merkava would have easy access to the engine compartment to afford quick battlefield maintenance and even replacement. According to reports, Tal and his design crew were adamant that, under battlefield conditions, the engine could be replaced in under 60 minutes.

Weaponry

The tank's design incorporated a low slope configuration into the hull and the turret design to decrease the angular impact of incoming anti-tank shells and missiles. The tank also possessed a rear escape hatch, which was not only useful for quick crew evacuation, but which could also be used to transport a few infantrymen, or keep a casualty comfortable and stable until he was transported to the battalion aid station. The large type of design utilised in the Merkava, compromising speed and mobility for protection, was in sharp contrast to the constricting size of the Soviet MBTs in Arab use; these tanks emphasised speed and mobility as part of the Soviet offensive doctrine of massive juggernaut attacks. The Merkava Mk I's main gun was the lethal 105mm M68 cannon, a weapon which since 1967 had destroyed thousands of Arab tanks. The primary concept behind the Merkava, however, and a trait that has followed all subsequent variants, is its armour protection and resiliency. The tank's *Migun* – armour protection – is layered all around the tank, with the tank's systems spread all around the crew and ammunition to provide extra protection, in addition to their operational intention. Three more factors contribute to the tank's resilience: the small silhouette of the tank in the fire position; the lack of flammable materials in the crew chambers; and the storage of the heavy ammunition under the turret ring.

THE BLUE AND WHITE MERKAVA

In May 1979, on Israel's 31st anniversary, the new and almighty 'Chariot' was unveiled in a stadium in Jerusalem during Independence Day celebrations. The new Merkava Mk I was as awe inspiring as it was powerful and revolutionary. Already, without it ever performing in combat or before the scrutiny of the press, it was labelled as the 'best tank in the world'. Its design was certainly unlike anything the Western military attachés had seen before. Many of the foreign tank officers, some flown to Israel especially to see the unveiling of the Merkava, were taken aback by the overall design of the tank. The low-sloped design reminded them of the Swedish S-Tank anti-tank vehicle, and the turret and crew placement in the vehicle's rear were completely new. As the tank was premiéred and the flash of correspondents' cameras illuminated the parade ground, the military attachés (as well as hundreds of IDF officers not involved in the Merkava project) were visably shocked to witness ten Israeli infantrymen, weighed down in full kit, suddenly emerge from the rear access door which was lowered by an internal hydraulic mechanism.

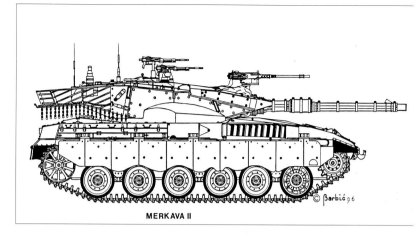

MERKAVA II

ABOVE **A 1:76 scale drawing of the Merkava Mk II. (Vasco Barbi**

Innovations in tank design

Many armoured warfare analysts were most impressed by the infantry-carrying ability of the Merkava, a truly revolutionary aspect of the tank's design. But carrying infantrymen into battle was just one extra feature of practical development that Tal had insisted upon. When designing the Merkava, Tal and his staff studied all the lessons learned in the 1967 and 1973 wars. They examined both Israeli conclusions, as well as examining reports from military intelligence about the Arab experience, too. Positive aspects were studied, as were negative points, and all facets of this study were incorporated in one way or another into the design pool. One of the most important studies from the 1973 War showed that Israeli tanks on the Golan and in Sinai tended to run out of ammunition faster than they could be re-supplied. It was crucial that the Merkava be

Churning through the mud and drainage ditches of a southern Israel training field, a Mk II awaits its turn on the 'live-fire' range. The photograph shows the frontal engine exhaust grate situated above the side-skirt armour, as well as a close-up of the fastening system used to 'secure' the side-skirt armour over the sensitive wheel suspension system. (Israeli MOD)

designed to carry a larger quantity of 105mm (or, even, possibly 120mm ordnance) so that individual tanks could fight extended battles without running out of rounds. The rear-storage compartment, usually the more secure portion of the tank, was an ideal ammunition hold. In special situations where an APC with a 105mm main armament gun was required, such as cross-border special operations forays, the additional ammunition could be removed and the troopers inserted, complete with their kit and specialised equipment.

Little information was provided about the Merkava's technical statistics at the time of its unveiling. It was considered a top-secret classified weapon system. Yet even though powered by the impressive Teledyne Continental AVDS-1790-6A V-12 diesel 900 horse-power engine, coupled to an Allison Transmission Division of General Motors, CD-850-6BX, the Merkava was built for combat and cautious fighting, not speed. The powerful power-plant was meant to push the hulking 62-ton vehicle through obstacle, up inclines and across the fields of the Golan Heights and the southern Lebanese valleys. To ensure that the tank did not require permanent field maintenance on its wheels and treads, Urdan Industries developed a special road wheel for the Merkava with twice the normal 'road life'. Six 790mm Centurion-type rubber-tyred wheels are suspended by helical springs and housed suspension arms.

Many observers were impressed, and even intrigued, by the revolutionary design. There was a multi-angle combination of welded and cast armour; much of the armoured protection is 'spaced', affording additional protection from HEAT and ATGW projectiles. The driver sits in the forward left side of the tank, and his access via his hatch or through the rear access door; the driver's visibility is afforded by three observation periscopes, and one that can be used for night-vision. The turret is also exceptional. All hydraulic gear and communications devices are located in the turret bustle and the tank commander (or *Ma'Tak* in the IDF/Hebrew slang) is positioned on the right portion of the turret; an optical sight (with a reported x4 to x20 power) mounted forward of his hatch provides a 360° line of vision. The gunner sits directly in front of the tank commander and his optical devices and sensory gear are positioned in the wedge-shaped right side of the turret; according to foreign reports, the gunner's optical sights have a magnification range of x8 and include a laser range-finder. The Mk I's 62 rounds of ammunition were carried in three distinct manners: six rounds were stored directly below the turret-ring in a ready-to-fire mode; 12 rounds were stored at the base of the rear hull in two-round containers, and the remaining 44 rounds were kept in special palletised four-round containers at the very rear of the tank.

BAPTISM OF FIRE IN THE LEBANON

When the Merkava was ready for actual deployment, the man who took the 'keys' from 'Talik' was Col. Avigdor Kahalani, commander of the 7th Brigade, and in 1973 recipient of Israel's highest medal for valour for his epic command of the 77th Battalion during the battle for the Valley of Tears on 9 October 1973. Although the Merkava was initially stationed on the Golan Heights across the 'Purple Line' facing Syrian positions on the other side of the frontier, the tank's baptism of fire came on 6 June

An excellent close-up view of the add-on armour plates positioned on the Merkava Mk II turret area. Although the Israeli Ministry of Defense remains tight-lipped about disclosing any details of the Merkava's armour protection, the photograph does provide a glimpse into its thickness and positioning. (IDF Spokesman)

1982, when tens of thousands of IDF troopers crossed Israel's northern border with Lebanon to initiate 'Operation Peace for Galilee.'

The operation's primary objective was the destruction of the Palestinian military presence in Lebanon, but war with Israel's traditional nemesis, Syria, was an inevitability, especially since the Syrians maintained over 30,000 troops throughout the country. Syria's surface-to-air missile batteries ringed the eastern portion of Lebanon, severely inhibiting Israeli air operations. When the IDF did, in fact, move on the Beka'a Valley, the Merkava reigned supreme. In the pitched and sometimes desperate battles of Sultan Ya'aqub and Ein Zehalta, the Merkava defeated everything the Syrians threw at it - armour, infantrymen and anti-tank helicopter gunships. Even the T-72, the latest Soviet tank in the Syrian arsenal, proved inferior to the armoured might of the IDF's Chariot. Against well-entrenched Palestinian forces armed with the capable RPG-7, and roaming Syrian commando teams equipped with Sagger and Milan ATGWs, the Merkava proved virtually impregnable; it led the columns of modified Centurion and M60 Pattons inexorably towards Beirut. In the Lebanon fighting, the 7th Brigade and its force of Merkavas faced off the T-72 in the Beka'a Valley. During the battle, the 7th Brigade destroyed eight T-72s at sniping ranges of 3,000 and 4,000 metres with its L7 105mm gun, while the T-72 in Syrian hands, with its 125mm main armament gun, failed to destroy a single Merkava. It is difficult in the context and

A daunting view of a platoon of Merkavas, from a particular battalion's 3rd platoon (note numeral 3 positioned on canvas marker on the rear of the rear-turret storage bin), patrolling a stretch of south Lebanon. Note how 105mm main armament cannons are pointed upward, at a slight inclination, aiming towards the hills favoured by Hizbollah guerrillas as launching pads for Sagger missile barrages. (IDF Spokesman)

space of this book to examine the tactical advantages afforded to Israeli commanders simply because the Merkava Mk I was in their order of battle, but the tank did have an incredible effect on the most important players in an armoured campaign – the tank soldiers who fight and die in the tanks. If the Merkava can be credited with any impact on the fighting, it is in the sense of security it provided to the crews who advanced with it up the coastal plain toward the Lebanese capital and through the Beka'a Valley onto the destructive clashes along the Beirut-Damascus Highway. 'You felt safe and protected inside the tank,' claimed one 7th Armored Brigade tank sergeant. 'Knowing that you would survive most hits allowed the commander, the gunner and the driver to

23

'concentrate on the task at hand, on destroying enemy tanks and hunting T-72s and BMPs as opposed to worrying about what ordnance was coming in your direction. Compared to the Centurion, the tank I was trained on, the electronic and aiming systems made the actual implementation of battle, hitting the enemy's tank dead centre on the first shot, a much easier exercise.'[1]

THE MK II & III's

A modified Mk II, with a typical smoke-grenade canisters positioned on either side of the 105mm main armament cannon. This system would be employed several years later on the Mk III variant. (Israeli MOD)

During the course of the 1982 Lebanon War, seven Merkavas were destroyed in the fighting and many others were damaged according to foreign reports, but the tank fulfilled its principal objective brilliantly. These same US military reports stated that all but one of the seven were destroyed by anti-tank mines, and one was hit by a barrage of RPG and Sagger fire. Although official IDF statistics remain classified, the percentage of tank soldiers killed in Merkava units, as opposed to those in Centurion and Patton units sporting Blazer reactive armour, was considerably lower. Along the coastal road linking Rosh Haniqra and Beirut, the Merkavas of Col. Eli Geva's 211th Armored Brigade suffered far fewer casualties than expected, even though they bore the brunt of dedicated - sometimes suicidal - Palestinian guerrilla anti-tank barrages consisting of ordnance ranging from RPG-7s and Saggers, to Chinese-produced recoilless rifles.

In the three months of 'conventional' combat in Lebanon between

A close-up look at the 'hook-on' side-skirt armour attachment system present on most Merkava Mk IIs. (IDF Spokesman)

---

1 Interview, Golan Heights, November 1992, Emeq Ha'Becha.

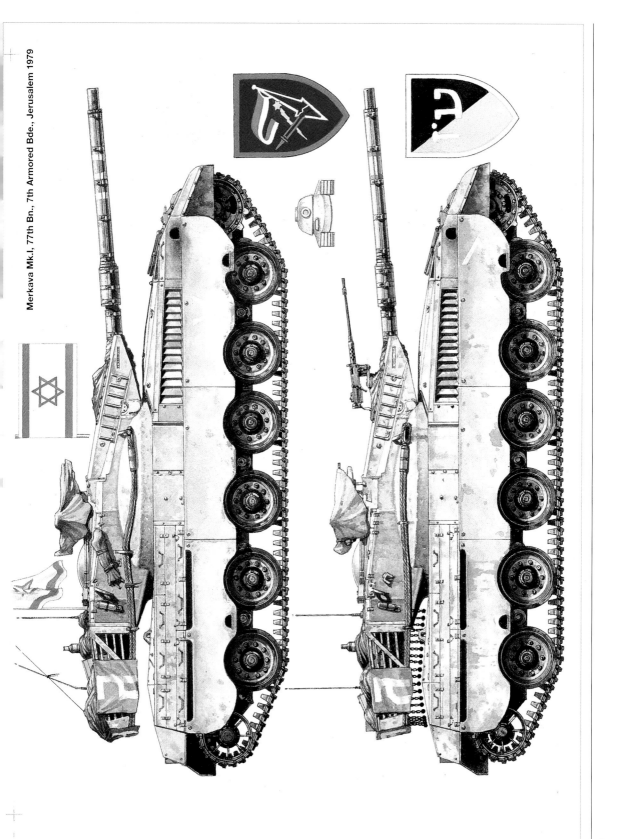

Merkava Mk.I, 77th Bn., 7th Armored Bde., Jerusalem 1979

A

Merkava Mk.I, 211th Armored Bde., Tyre, Lebanon, 1982

B

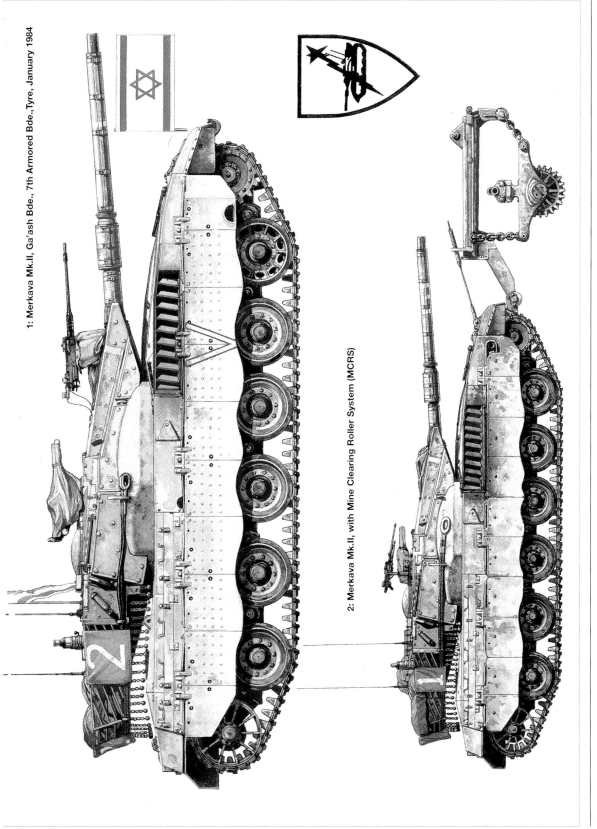

1: Merkava Mk.II, Ga'ash Bde., 7th Armored Bde., Tyre, January 1984

2: Merkava Mk.II, with Mine Clearing Roller System (MCRS)

MERKAVA MK.II
MARJAYOUN, SOUTHERN LEBANON, AUGUST 1985

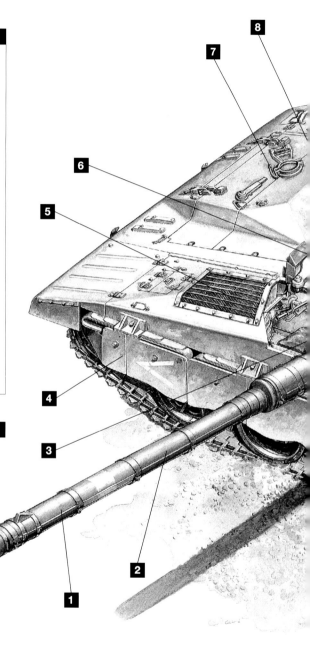

KEY

1 Thermal sleeve
2 L7/ M68 105mm main armament
3 Driver's compartment
4 Side-skirt armour
5 Engine vent for Teledyne Continental AVDS-1790-6A
6 Driver's hatch
7 105mm gun mount
8 Teledyne Continental AVDS-1790-6A V12 diesel 900 horse power engine
9 Forward gun-base mounted .50 calibre heavy machine gun
10 60mm mortar
11 Commander's 7.62mm (modified) FN MAG light machine gun
12 Commander's sights
13 Commander's cupola/ hatch
14 Main gun loading port
15 Antenna
16 Gunner's communication system
17 Gunner's perch
18 Orange identificational sheet
19 Crew's extra stowage
20 Fire extinguisher
21 Rear turret 'ball and chain' defensive mechanism
22 Gunner's 7.62mm (modified) FN MAG light machine gun
23 Towing lines
24 Crew's medical gear
25 Stretcher
26 Rear access door
27 Rear ammunition storage bin
28 Rear access communication port
29 Crew's stored gear
30 Road wheel
31 Ammunition storage bin
32 Ammunition carousel storage area

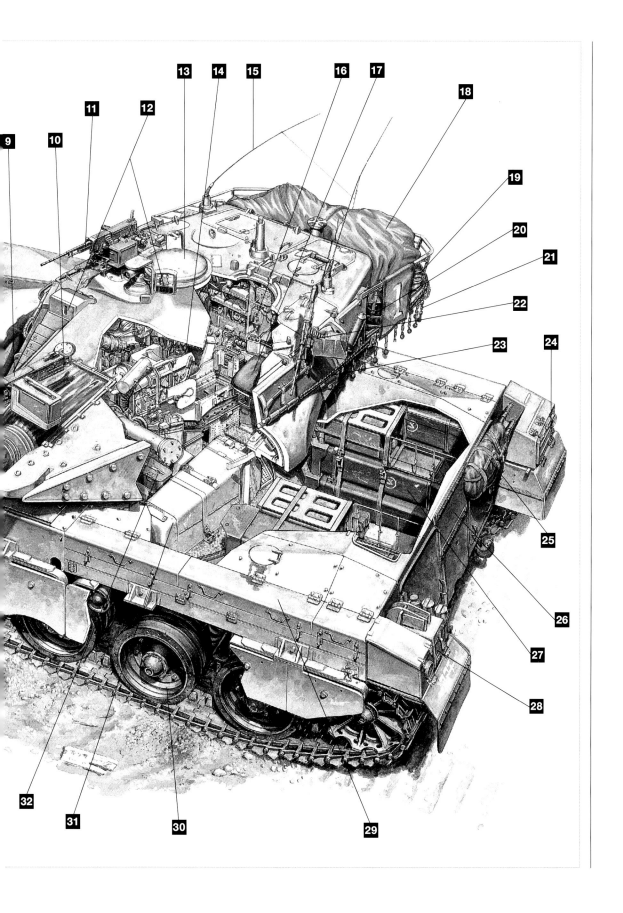

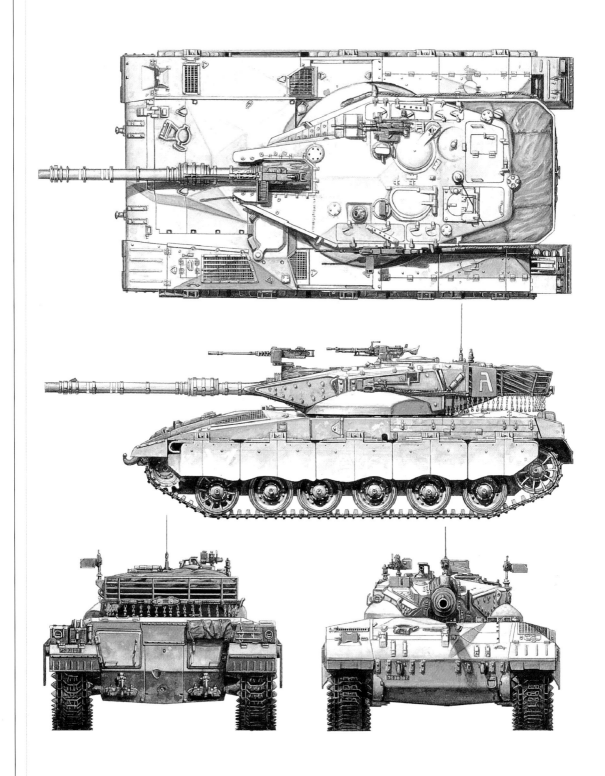

Merkava Mk.II, 188th 'Barak' Armored Bde., Golan Heights, 1986

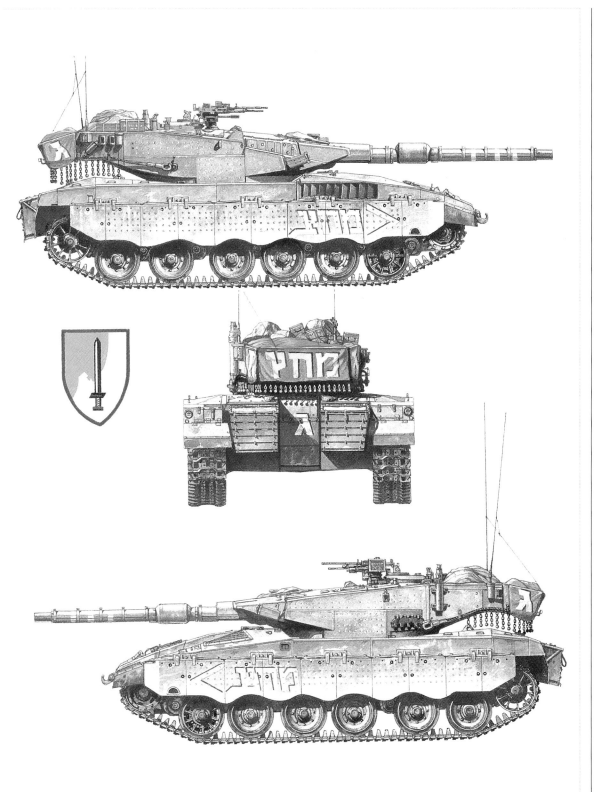

Merkava Mk.III, 188th 'Barak' Armored Bde., Northern Israel, 1990

F

Merkava Mk.III, Further information is classified

A tank crew from the 7th Armored Brigade performs emergency maintenance on their Mk II during a Northern Command competition on the Golan Heights. Note engine exhaust panels, and mount for the gun-base-mounted .50 cal. heavy machine gun. (IDF Spokesman)

June and September 1982, only a handful of Merkava crewmen became battlefield fatalities in the pitched battles of Ein el-Hilweh, Sultan Ya'aqub and the Beirut–Damascus Highway. General Tal's vision had struck pay dirt.

New modifications

As the Merkavas in various brigades were fighting it out against Syrian armour in the Beka'a Valley and against the PLO along the coast of Beirut, 'Talik' and his round table of armoured warfare experts were busy at work placing the finishing touches on the next generation of Merkava, the Mk II. The lessons of the Lebanon conflict were analysed carefully and incorporated into the next model's design. Crews who had fought in tank-versus-tank battles were interviewed and asked what suggestions they would make if they were working on the Merkava project. Of course, any tank battle you can walk away from is a good one, so the Mk I received positive reviews in its safety features and handling. The narrow confines of Lebanon's mountain roads did make manoeuvrability a concern, but the Merkava production team could not make the tank any narrower, nor could they design a tank to accommodate close-quarter urban fighting; after all, some argued, 'Operation Peace for Galilee' was supposed to be the IDF's first and last Lebanon campaign. Studies found that the majority of Merkavas hit and destroyed in Lebanon were actually hit from behind, in the tank's soft 'backside-

A close-up view of the Mk II turret, including the mortar slot seen right below the loader's cupola. (IDF Spokesman)

underbelly' where the turret and chassis presented a diagonal squared target underneath the rear storage bin. It was here, Tal's studies found, that anti-tank ordnance, such as Saggers and RPGs, were able to penetrate the Merkava turret and inflict death and destruction on the crew. As a result, a revolutionary ball and chain configuration was added to the rear turret of the

The mightiest Merkava of them all – the Mk III, unveiled in the summer of 1989. (Israeli MOD)

Merkava Mk II for added protection against AT projectiles, primarily HEAT rounds, aimed at the sensitive crux between turret and chassis. While many tank experts called this contraption 'a poor man's reactive armour kit', the inexpensive and basically pragmatic configuration was incredibly effective. During test trials at firing ranges in central Israel it was discovered that the balls and chain presented a deceptive armour crunch-point for anti-tank ordnance fired at that spot, and rounds tended to detonate on the balls instead of a few centimetres further against the turret. Studies also revealed that even though Merkava crews knew that their tanks were among the world's top in terms of crew protection, crews who had been in combat and come face-to-face with a Syrian T-72's 125mm anti-tank round *always* felt insecure. As a result, the design team of the Merkava Mk II opted to improve the turret's armour protection with add-on armour plates, though the exact thickness and configuration of this add-on design has never been released by the security-conscious Israelis; some foreign reports claim that these plates are reactive Blazer-type additions. Special armour plates were also attached to the hull.

In addition to these turret improvements, an advanced electronic

Right off the assembly line and awaiting its new owners from the 188th Barak Brigade, a Mk III is displayed without its side-skirt armour attached. Note how the basic skeletal design is quite similar to the Mk I and Mk II, though once fully equipped with all its add-on elements, it becomes a tank of a completely different dimension. (Israeli MOD)

system capable of withstanding the strongest of impacts by enemy
ordnance was redesigned and put in place throughout the turret. The
Mk II variant was equipped with a modified Neodymium laser range-
finder and a more advanced fire-control computer system. Other noted
developments on the Mk II included increased mobility and speed (with
an indigenously produced transmission that enabled the Mk II to double
its range to 500 kilometres), as well as the inclusion of an internal com-
mander-operated 60mm mortar. Mounted on the left side of the turret,
the handy mortar was positioned so that it could be loaded and fired
from within an enclosed turret.

Mine clearing and air defence modifications

During the 1982 Lebanon fighting, one of the most daunting enemy
defences encountered by the 7th Armored Brigade in the Beka'a Valley
was a road-blocking obstacle littered with anti-personnel and anti-tank
mines. During the IDF's armoured push through the Beka'a Valley, the
narrow and winding mountain arteries were often only wide enough for

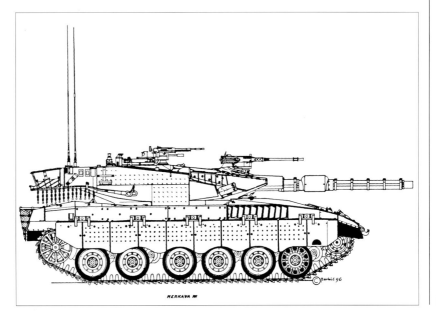

MERKAVA III

Frontal view of the Mk III and its 120mm main armament gun. Of interesting note is a sensor, of unknown type, situated below the mount for the gun-base .50 cal. machine gun (not yet affixed when this photograph was taken). Most aspects of the Mk III are still considered classified top-secret by the IDF. (Israeli MOD)

one tank to pass. When t? vehicles were confronted obstacles, either abandon? tanks ringed with explosi? or fallen trees littered wi? mines, the advan? sometimes stopped for long as six hours. Ma? times, engineering vehic? couldn't even reach th source of the bottlene? because of the narrown? of the roadways, and as result much of the da? gerous clearing work had be done by hand. Syri? tank crews and Palestini? guerrillas often used the traffic jams as perfe? opportunities to laun? anti-tank ambushes. Syrian tank units, hidden in the peaks above t? road, would unleash 115mm rounds and then depart, or else RPG a? Sagger teams (either Syrian commandos or PLO squads) would cre? down from the hills, hide behind trees and bush, and empty their loads anti-tank ordnance before racing back into the wilderness.

As a result, another major addition and modification to the Merka? Mk IIs were bolts and fasteners capable of carrying either a bulldoz? blade or mine-destroying rollers. The Israeli defence industry began pr? ducing high-endurance bulldozer blades that could sweep roadsi? obstacles away (as well as absorb the impact of explosives) and cou? easily be attached to Merkava MBTs. Mk Is were modified and equippe? with these engineering devices, as were the later production Mk IIs. ? addition, an intricate and highly successful anti-mine rolling device w? developed, with penetrating teeth that could simply pounce over minefield and clear a narrow, though sometimes vital, path over a boob? trapped stretch of earth. In their deployments in southern Lebano? inside the security zone where Hizbollah ambushes were commonplac? these devices proved to be invaluable.

Maj.-Gen. Tal and his design team also interviewed tank crews to a? them what improvements they felt were needed to the Mk II variant whi? entered production in late 1983. One of the more daunting a? destructive challenges that Israeli tank and APC crews encountered Lebanon was the helicopter gunship. Over the Beka'a Valley, and t? Beirut–Damascus Highway, Aérospatiale SA 342 Gazelles and Mi-24 Hin? flying the Syrian Air Force tricolour proved that, in many ways, they rul? the tree-lines of Lebanon. Capable of launching their HOT and Swatt? from ranges beyond those of the Israeli's turret-mounted 7.62mm and .? cal. machine guns, Syrian tank-killing choppers were able to snipe away Israeli mechanised columns, launch their ordnance from protecti? ranges, and then return to bases inside Syria for refuelling and reloadin? Many tank crews, upon hearing the 'rat-a-tat' whooshing of a? approaching Syrian chopper shuddered in fear. Many found it difficult

action realising that they might fall target to the airborne launched
nk-killers; according to some interviewees, even tank commanders
ind it daunting to stand upright in their turret and fire their machine
ns at the menacing gunships. As a result, many Merkava Mk IIs were
uipped with two 7.62mm FN MAG light machine guns for the com-
inder and loader, and a .50 cal. heavy machine gun positioned at the
ry base of the 105mm gun so that a crewman lying down could engage
emy aircraft from a more secure and accurate (not to mention com-
table!) firing position. The forward positioned .50 cal. gun was most
eful in the counter-guerrilla operations that Merkava units embarked
on in the IDF-Hizbollah campaign in southern Lebanon in late 1983,
en the first Mk IIs were produced. This campaign continues in the
curity zone at the time of writing. Some Merkava Mk IIs, especially those
rving inside the South Lebanon security zone, have had US-built Mk 19
mm grenade launchers mounted near the loader's hatch instead of the
ual MAG or .50 cal. gun.

Production of the Merkava Mk II continued until 1989 and the tank
w limited action in southern Lebanon, primarily on infantry support
signments against Hizbollah terrorists armed with Saggers and RPGs.
engagements where the Mk II units were fired upon with anti-tank
dnance, the new protective measures proved both invaluable and
pervious. When it came time to develop and design the Merkava Mk
, Maj.-Gen. Tal and his staff of armour officers and engineers realised
at Israel could not design and develop a new tank every decade or so
such a luxury was economically impossible for a nation and defence
dustry as small as Israel's. In reality, there was no need to abandon the
iginal Merkava design concept, either. The Mk I variant served the
mored Corps brilliantly in Lebanon and the Mk II had been a faithful
nk serving in the best tank brigades in the Armored Corps' order of
ttle. Crews were quite fond of the Mk II's performance, and com-
anders had scored high points for their tank units on exercises and on

anoeuvres. Yet in reality,
e Mk II was a stop-gap
grade of the initial
rsion of the design, not
overall improvement.
aj.-Gen. Tal wanted to
ild a brand new tank on
existing platform, one
corporating improved
epower, improved
obility and improved
chnology. The drawing
ard stage of the Mk III's
velopment began several
eks after the first Mk II's
lled out of the IMI
ctory door in August
83.

Looking at the
anging face of the
iddle Eastern military

map in 1983, Maj.-Gen. Tal viewed an Arab world equipping its armed forces with the world's most powerful and technologically superior MBTs on the market. The Syrians, the Iraqis and the Iranians all fielded T-72s; the Jordanians had the mighty updated Chieftain (the 'Khalid'); the Saudis boasted the French AMX-30, and even the tiny United Arab Emirates had the Italian-produced OF-40. Peace existed with Egypt, but the Egyptian Army still fielded thousands of T-62s and M60s, and there were rumours of the US selling the Mubarak regime the powerful M1 Abrams. These vehicles were almost exclusively equipped with newly developed armoured skeletons, and upgraded armour protection far superior to that of the MBTs that fought in the 1973 War and, indeed, in Lebanon. As a result, Maj.-Gen. Tal's first point of improvement in the Mk III variant would be improved firepower and a substitute for the L7/M68 105mm rifled gun.

Improved firepower and technological advances

The L7/M68 105mm rifled gun had been, perhaps, the true unsung hero in Israel's wars of 1967, 1973 and 1982; certainly the gun had resulted in nearly 1,000 enemy deaths. Yet in spite of the new and improved APFSDS ammunition that had been specifically developed for the L7/M68, Maj.-Gen. Tal realised that the time had come for the IDF to introduce a larger cal. main armament gun. Imagining a worse case scenario, 'Talik' did not want Israeli brigades on the Golan Heights using the 105mm gun to shoot it out against T-80s equipped with Soviet copies of the Israeli-designed Blazer armour. The 120mm gun seemed to be most suitable to the initial blueprints, though the weapon would have to be designed and built inside Israel; initial consideration, briefly, centred on a licence arrangement with the American producers of the M256 120mm gun serving on the M1s, but this defeated the very purpose of a completely indigenously produced tank. 'Talik' wanted every screw, every bolt, every cannon on 'his' tank to be made in the Jewish State.

There were other considerations behind the decision to arm the Mk III variant with a 120mm gun. Producing an indigenous gun was one thing, but an arms production industry that for years had developed, designed and produced 105mm ammunition would now have to change gear and begin the production of an advanced line of 120mm ammunition. Selecting a gun of the same calibre as that on the main American tank in US Army service, the M1, meant that should full-scale war erupt once again in the Middle East, with the IDF forced to rely on an American arms lift, then the USA would be able to supply the IDF with plentiful stores of 120mm ammunition. The tank, for purposes of pride and political necessity, needed to be made solely in Israel – ammunition could always be purchased on the open market.

With an improved weapon of larger calibre, 'Talik' realised that the Mk III would not be able to carry so much ammunition, partly because the 120mm shells were larger, but also because they required additional protection. Carrying less ammunition was a trade-off in the eyes of the Mk III design team: if the gun was more powerful and capable of decimating its target on the first shot, supported by an even more advanced fire-control system, then less ammunition would not specifically hinder the vehicle's battlefield performance. The 120mm ammunition would be carried in specially designed fire-retardant canisters, providing the

One of the first production-line Mk IIIs during its initial test-firing exercises in southern Israel. The photograph shows the modified shape and design of the Mk III, turret including the panels of the classified armour fixed around the turret skeleton infra- structure. Note how the battalion marking is painted on side-skirt armour, and not stencilled on. (Israeli MOD)

crew with an extra edge of protection should the tank's armour be pen- etrated by a HEAT or KE round. Studies of Israeli tanks destroyed on the battlefields of Sinai and the Golan, as well as in Lebanon in 1982, indicated that a fair percentage – too high a number to be ignored – of Armored Corps fatalities were from stored ammunition that detonated in the initial tank fire.

By 1983 Israel's 'Silicon Valley' computer research firms, nestled in a strip near the northern port city of Haifa, had evolved from a small high- tech community into world players on the computer and advanced electronic field. Many of these firms, with names like Rafael, Elbit, Elscint and El-Op, were dedicated to Israel's growing defence industry and many were enlisted to provide systems for the first two Merkava variants; they were called upon again for the Mk III.

The most important high-tech aspect of the Mk III was the fire- control system – the *Bakar Esh* as it is known in Hebrew. The Mk III's fire-control system was a joint venture between Elbit and El-Op, and incorporated a laser range finder, a fire-control computer, and a day/night sighting system available to both the tank commander and the gunner. For the first time, this new system enabled an Israeli tank to accurately fire on the move with the inclusion of a line-of-sight stabili- sation system for both the gunner and commander. Being able to fire on the move is valuable for any tank, as it eliminates the need to stop, search for cover, and acquire enemy targets. The high-tech features of the post- 1982 tanks permitted all these functions while rolling at top speed. This aspect of tank warfare is vital when fighting in the vast open expanses of the desert, and it is clear that the Mk III was designed with Israel's next war (one fought against Iraq or Iran, perhaps) in mind. While the IDF Armored School liked to boast that it produced the best tank com- manders in the business, as well as the most accurate gunners, the now legendary *Tzalafim* (snipers) of the 7th Brigade, there are factors beyond those taught in a classroom that make an accurate gunner. To ensure

that each 120mm unleashed by the Mk III would hit its mark, the fire-control system's advanced (and highly classified) ballistic computer was incorporated with alphanumeric displays showing all meteorological, climatic and elevation movements and conditions.

The Merkava Mk III is the first tank in the world equipped with an operational electromagnetic threat warning system with hemispherical coverage. Foreign defence analysts who were permitted to examine the Merkava when first unveiled, reported that four sensor elements were installed on the turret's front section, two on the rear port, and one each on the starboard sides; as a result of these placements, the Merkava Mk III enjoys 360° coverage.

Maj.-Gen. Tal believed that the tank always possessed a considerable and sometimes understated edge when faced with an infantry anti-tank threat. He held the view that the tank, no matter what the scenario, was always a tank's greatest battlefield threat, but he also realised that enemy infantry formations needed to be countered. In the Mk II version of the Merkava, this was achieved by mounting two FN MAG 7.62mm light machine guns on the turret, along with a .50 cal. heavy machine gun, all augmented by a 60mm mortar inside the turret. Indeed, the mortar was one of the most popular weapons according to surveys of tank crews in units equipped with the Mk II. Units deployed to southern Lebanon during joint-security operations and retaliatory strikes have found the mortar incredibly effective in an anti-infantry role, and especially good in launching flares; in many cases, 60mm flare rounds were effective in blinding enemy infra-red night vision equipment. It should, however, be noted that smoke dischargers are fitted to the exterior of the Mk III turret enabling a cloud of protective cover at a moment's notice even if the crew is busy firing the 60mm in an anti-personnel mission.

New armoured shell design

Beyond firepower, the second most important improvement in the Mk III variant was to be in armour protection and in this regard Maj.-Gen. Tal opted to be truly revolutionary. Inherently frugal and practical,

Merkava Component Manufacturers

The overall Israeli industrial support for the Merkava Mk III project is best expressed in the number of companies enlisted in the tank's production. Among the components produced by different indigenous defence industries, are:

- Israel Military Industries: 120mm main armament gun; smoke-screen system final drive; idler wheel mechanism; road wheel suspension; traverse gear box; and turret ring

- Urdan Industries Ltd.:   hull front and deck; turret main body; gun shield; gun mount; turret basket; suspension idler wheels; sprocket wheels; and sprockets and housing

- Soltam Ltd.:   commander's hatch; 60mm mortar

- Pladot: air inlet and exhaust system

- Betihut Franz Levi Ltd.:   fuel tanks

- Yail Noa: air inlet sector; peritelescope mount

- Metalworks Ltd.:   braking, steering, gearshift and accelerator system; commander's machine gun mount

- MTLM Carmiel: commander's, gunner's, and loader's seat

- Shalom Chemical Industries Ltd.:   NBC System

- Dadon: crew seats; loader's hatch

- Sabaco: commander's hatch; crew's seats

- Palbam: water and fuel containers

- EL-OP Electro-Optics Industries Ltd.:   commander's day/night sight; driver's peritelescope; and llaser range-finder.

- Spectronix Ltd.:   fire extinguishing and suppression system

- Elbit Computers Ltd.:   tank fire control system

- Orlite engineering Co. Ltd.:   ammunition and grenade containers

- Vidco Ltd.:   thermal sleeve

- Krimolovsky: ballistic shield

- Israel Aircraft Industries Ltd.:   shock absorbers; gunner's control; hydraulic power pack; stabiliser; ballistic drive

- Tadiran: communications system

- Amcoram: commander's zoom sight control; pedal

Israelis often think of equipment in two ways: 'How can I use it now, and how can I improve it in the future for a minimum price?' The Mk I version of the Merkava was a 'what you see is what you get' tank, as was the Mk II; in essence, they were examples of built-in obsolescence, victims of ever-increasing technology in the arms race, even though they were more than capable lethal fighting systems. Maj.-Gen. Tal wanted to ensure that the Mk III could adapt to survive, and designed a modular armour protection system. Instead of the traditional cast or welded armour found on most earlier tanks, the Mk III would incorporate an interior skeleton and a modular outer shell that could be removed and replaced with the latest developments in armour technology. The new modular plates would be bolted to the tank's hull and exterior turret shell instead of being welded on or cast completely through. This pragmatic development, Tal argued, would be useful on two counts: firstly, if there was a new breakthrough in armoured steel technology, the existing exterior shell could simply be removed and replaced; secondly, and more importantly during war, damaged or destroyed chunks of armour could be replaced at battalion repair stations by Ordnance Corps crew. The turnaround for returning a damaged vehicle to the front could be cut from the usual 48 hours of frantic work to an astounding six hours.

The first test of this design came with the *Ma'Ga'Ch 7*, the Israeli-upgraded M60 that was equipped with a modular turret and hull reinforcement in late 1988. Even though the modular design was inked into the blueprints for the Mk III as far back as 1985, little information is available on the composite nature of the modular armour as it remains one of the most closely guarded secrets in Israel. No information has been released as to the spacing of the armour, or the nature of its design, though it is known that the modular sheets are passive, and not Blazer-type reactive armour. The foreign defence media, who were offered close access to the Merkava Mk I and Mk II, have been kept far away from a close examination of the Mk III.

Special add-on armour skirts support the upper half of the wheels and suspensions, and the engine area and the frontal turret are well sloped to withstand a frontal attack by providing unique angle silhouettes. Yet the Merkava wouldn't be a Merkava if the front compartment of the tank, the frontal arc and engine compartment, weren't protected more than the tank's other areas. If the armour is penetrated and the round manages to overcome the difficult penetration angle provided by the sloped hull and turret, the engine compartment and the stored diesel fuel provide an ample shield to prevent any conventional AT shell from entering the crew's compartment.

Special protective features

If an anti-tank round actually does penetrate part of the Merkava Mk III's armour, specific safety tripwires have been incorporated into the vehicles basic design. 'Prevention is worth an ounce of cure in tank-versus-tank warfare,' claims one senior IDF tank officer, and as a result Maj.-Gen. Tal saw to it that the Mk III was equipped with a newly developed, indigenously produced, electromagnetic warning device that alerts the crew the moment their vehicle is fixed in a laser beam from an enemy tank, infantry anti-tank team or even a tank-killing chopper, such as the Hind or Gazelle. To minimise the chances of an in-turret fire should a round penetrate the armoured protection, the volatile hydraulic system found in many Western-built tanks (including the Merkava Mk I and Mk II) has been replaced with an electronic turret control. A high-tech and classified fire-prevention (detection and suppression) system is also built in to the Mk III version, including ammunition storage tubes that maintain a specifically low temperature throughout the tank's deployment. NBC protection in the Mk III, an important consideration before the Gulf War in view of the heavy investment into the biological and chemical agents by the Syrians, Iraqis and Iranians, is complete when the over-pressurised interior is battened down.

As the 188th Barak Brigade incorporates the Merkava Mk III into its ranks, Maj.-Gen. Tal is busy working on the next generation of 'Chariot', one ready for the technological combat of the next century. Already, in the Mk III variant, tank warfare as Israelis have come to know it has already gone high-tech. 'In the Merkava Mk III the tank commander is

tasked with having an accelerated thinking process enabling him to meet all the technological options,' claimed 'Talik' in an interview with the Israel Defense Force magazine. 'Because of the Mk III's ability to traverse all terrain conditions at high speeds, the commander and crew's element of time has increased markedly, requiring better instinctive and reactionary skills.'[2]

Improved speed and manoeuvrability

In contrast to comparable vehicles on the market, the Merkava Mk I and Mk II were considered slow movers - they were large, heavy, and could never reach a speed surpassing 46 kmh (the M1 Abrams, for example, could reach a top speed of 72.4 kmh; Germany's Leopard 2 could hit 72 kmh; the T-72 was capable of 60 kmh, as was the Khalid). Both versions of the Merkava were built specifically for the battlefields of the Golan Heights and southern Lebanon, mountainous stretches of treacherous fighting ground where a tank weighing over 60 tons couldn't even reach high speeds without slamming into a boulder or being driven off a twisting road. The Mk III was a tank for a different type of warfare. Maj.-Gen. Tal realised that Israel's next major war (or even protracted conflict) need not be restricted to the Valley of Tears, (again) or even the Beka'a Valley. The next major war would be a fast, offensive one with less strategic depth than before, and the need to push the battle as far away from Israel's frontiers as possible. Although the maximum speed of the Mk III remains classified, the 900 horsepower engine found in both the Mk I and Mk II versions has been considerably upgraded to a Teledyne Continental AVDS-1790-9AR 12,000hp 12-cycle air-cooled turbo-charged diesel engine. To improve mobility, especially over the boulder-strewn wasteland of the Golan Heights and southern Lebanon, specially modified shock absorbers have been added to the tank's ballistic steel suspension system.

Israeli tank officers, including those who have seen the best American, British and French tanks close up, swear that the Merkava Mk III is the finest and most powerful tank available anywhere in the world, especially when in the hands of the Israeli tank soldier. 'The human touch in the

2 Leak Ashat, *'Ha'Merkava Siman 4 Tehiye Kfitzat Madrega Nosefet,'* Bamachane, October 30, 1991, p. 53.

tank is the hands that bring the machine from its parked state to a mobile and lethal fighting machine,' claims one commander of the 188th Barak Armored Brigade's 'Receive' Battalion, the first tank unit in Israel to deploy the Mk III. 'The Merkava is a technologically superior tank and as a result requires the crew and commanders to provide quicker reflexes and judgement calls.' Because of the challenges imposed by the Mk III, the IDF Armored Corps did not want to place its newest, most powerful and most expensive tank in the hands of just any soldiers. It wanted this new 'baby', as the tank is referred to in Armored Corps circles, to be deployed among the best soldiers in the brigade. The brightest, most capable and most motivated tank soldiers, gunners, loaders, drivers and commanders were removed from other platoons and companies and channelled into an élite cadre of ground breakers who would inaugurate the vehicle into the IDF''s order of battle. Following the 1973 War, when the soldiers of 7th Brigade became national heroes, the IDF General Staff felt that the 188th Barak Brigade, an élite tank unit in its own right, had been unfairly overlooked. After the 7th Brigade's 'average' performance in Lebanon in 1982, it was decided that the next major honour that the IDF had to offer a tank unit would go to the 188th – a unit that had suffered over 75 per cent casualties in 1973.

MK IV AND BEYOND

On the eve of Israel's 41st Independence Day, in the spring of 1989, the first Merkava Mk III was handed over to Col. Eyal, the 188th Brigade commander, in a solemn ceremony on the Golan Heights. Senior tank officers, those first taught in the Patton or Centurion, are tremendous admirers of the Merkava Mk III, although they are still nostalgic for the old days when tanks were smaller and less technological. Maj.-Gen. Tal, the man who has, from day one been at the centre of the Merkava project, is busy at work completing the details on the Mk IV. Although security around the Mk IV project has been unprecedented, news reports in such publications as *Jane's Defence Weekly* have suggested that

Merkava Tank Comparisons

	Mk I	Mk II	Mk III
Weight (tons)	63	63	62
Main Gun (mm)	105	105	120
Ammunition Cap.	62 rounds	62 rounds	50 rounds
Machine Guns	3	3	3
60mm Mortar	external	internal	internal
Engine (HP)	900	900	1200
Transmission	semi-automatic	automatic, electronic control	automatic, electronic control
Suspension	1st generation	1st generation	2nd generation
Fire Control System	electronic computer, laser range-finder, night vision system	modern electronic computer, modern laser range-finder, modern night vision system	modern electronic computer, modern laser range-finder, modern night vision system, stabilised vertical and horizontal line of sight
Turret Control	electro-hydraulic	electro-hydraulic	electric and manual
Ballistic Protection	all-round spaced armour	combined spaced armour and add-on plates	modular special armour
Ammunition Survivability	heat resistant	heat resistant	heat resistant and chain detonation resistant
NBC System	over-pressurised fighting compartment	over-pressurised fighting compartment	high over-pressurised fighting compartment, central filter, crew air conditioning
Electromagnetic Warning System	elementary and basic	elementary and basic	classified

possible improvements could include a larger calibre gun or electro-thermal weaponry. Whatever the Mk IV will carry into battle, Maj.-Gen. Tal promises soon to unveil a Merkava that will once again boggle the imagination and lay claim to the title of the world's most powerful main battle tank.

To date, the Merkava Mk III has yet to be blooded in full-scale tank-versus-tank action, and the designers of the tank, all Armored Corps veterans, want to keep it that way. The closest that the tank came to seeing full-scale combat was, according to foreign reports, during the Gulf War of 1991. The Gulf War, in fact, has had an incredible impact on Israeli armoured thinking; planners have seen how the emphasis has shifted from border conflicts to possible regional deployments. The September 1993 peace agreement with the Palestine Liberation Organisation, and the October 1994 peace treaty with the Hashemite Kingdom of Jordan, has made the State of Israel truly a regional player in both economic development and in the area's overall security. While it is impossible to predict another large-scale war in the region, the August 1995 deployments of Iraqi forces against both Jordan and Kuwait proved yet again that the area is a tinderbox waiting to ignite. As a result, Israel's armoured forces need not only be better than her immediate neighbours, but the best in the entire region.

THE PLATES

A: Merkava Mk I, 77th Bn., 7th Armored Bde., Jerusalem 1979

When the IDF unveiled the first Merkava to a crowd of dignitaries and Armored Corps veterans, the impact of this new vision of steel and ballistic firepower was overwhelming. So complete had the IDF veil of secrecy been over the Merkava project, that few outside General Tal's inner circle knew what to expect when the vehicle was displayed on the 31st anniversary of Israeli independence in May 1979. Both tanks are adorned in the 'out-of-the-factory' greyish-sand scheme, belonging to the 7th Armored Brigade's 77th 'Oz' or ('Courage') Battalion, the same tank unit that fought off the Syrian juggernaut in the Valley of Tears during the 1973 War. The modified version seen above is adorned with the Israeli flag. Alongside it is an Armoured Corps metal clasp, the 7th Brigade unit symbol for ceremonial display, and below it the Battalion insignia. Note that the storage bin usually found to the rear of the Merkava turret was only placed on the tanks in 1981.

B: Merkava Mk I, 211th Armored Bde., Tyre, Lebanon, July 1982

This Mk I from Col. Eli Geva's 211th Brigade (according to published accounts) shows a distinct difference to the pristine model first displayed in the Jerusalem stadium in 1979 – four days of war in the Lebanon chaos will 'weather'

any vehicle. In typical IDF fashion, the Merkavas went to war adorned with a hodgepodge of crew equipment and extra geared stowed both in the overflowing bin, as well as attached around the turret. This tank is equipped with a turret-mounted Israeli-produced FN MAG 7.62mm light machine guns. (Whether or not a vehicle deployed a .50 cal heavy machine gun was usually dependent on crew preference or on the likelihood of an attack by enemy anti-tank helicopter gunships.) Shown with it are the Armored Corps banner (green and black), and above it the metal badge worn by Armored Corpsmen.

C1: Merkava Mk II, Ga'ash Bn., 7th Armored Bde., Tyre, January 1984

When Israeli soldiers were despatched into Lebanon, they never dreamed that they would be stuck in Lebanon for one winter, let alone two for that matter. Winters in Lebanon were nothing like those experienced by most soldiers in Israel, and consisted of bone-biting cold, occasional snow blizzards and an almost daily barrage of shivering rain. The roadways and fields of the country were turned into a seasonal mud pool making any military operations an absolute nightmare, especially for tank crews who were forced to clean the mud from their vehicles. The weather tended to hinder aggressive IDF

BELOW **Brigadier-General Yossi Ben-Hanan, hero of the 1973 War, and at the time of this photograph in 1988 the IDF Chief Armor Officer, inspects a Mk II crew and their tank with support bulldozer blade attachment. (IDF Spokesman)**

patrols and security operations considerably; as a result, tank units were usually moved into position in support of infantry squads on the march, with the tanks' 105mm main armament gun used for fire support and their night-fighting equipment for intelligence support. As can be seen on this Merkava Mk operating in the muddy nightmare of a Tyre byway, the tank commander's FN MAG 7.62mm light machine gun is fitted with an American-produced AN/PVS-4 night scope. Because of the mud that usually engulfed forward encampment tents, crews tended to store all their kit on top of their tanks in the hope that it would stay dry. Note the added arnour plating, and the defensive ball and chain arrangement to the rear of the turret - one of the most visible improvements made on the Mk II variant, though enhanced electronics and fire-control were also important developments.

C2: This tank has the MCRS (Mine Clearing Roller System) attached to its hull. The MCRS was most useful during operational assignments in Lebanon in the post-1985 war against Hizbollah, when land-mines were used to great effective. Israelis look at their most modern weapons platforms as unfinished canvases that can always be modified. They conceive, invent and produce 'innovative' additions to existing systems, be it a McDonnell Douglas F-4 Phantom or an indigenously produced Merkava Mk II. This bulldozer attachment had practical applications beyond clearing guerrilla ambushes. Seen alongside is the battalion emblem, usually stenciled on the tank.

D: Interior of Merkava Mk II, Marjayoun, Southern Lebanon. August 1985

Designed to be a survivable main-battle tank in the target rich environment of all-out tank versus tank warfare, the Merkava proved itself a capable patrol vehicle and APC in the RPG and Sagger saturated battlefield of counter-insurgency warfare. As seen here, the Merkava's design makes it an ideal combat vehicle for slicing paths for patrolling infantry in terrain where ATGW ambushes would stop most tanks; the three turret mounted guns as much for anti-aircraft use, as they are for providing massive .50 calibre and 7.62mm attention to infantry threats. Note the vehicle's spacious interior, and access to the rear cargo/ infantry hold area.

E: Merkava Mk II, 188th 'Barak' Armored Bde., Golan Heights 1986

Great strides have been made in the decoration of Israeli tanks in recent years, the pattern going from only the barest of markings to fully-fledged battalion, company, platoon and even squad insignia. This tank, from the Hermon Battalion, Aleph or A Company, Second Platoon (as evident from the Aleph/2 marking placed on the rear turret storage bin on a khaki canvas sheet) is featured as it would be seen on patrol

or on manoeuvres on the Golan Heights, the area of operation for the 188th Brigade, 'eyeball-to-eyeball' with the Syrians. If the IDF learned anything from the bitter battles waged in the Lebanon, it was the fact that a helicopter gunship, with long-range anti-tank guidance munitions, could wreak untold havoc on advancing armoured columns. As a result of the Lebanon experience, IDF tanks, Merkavas included, were soon adorned with double (even triple) turret mounted light and heavy machine guns. The .50 cal. heavy machine gun, perhaps the most effective such weapon ever produced, was found to be particularly effective against incoming helicopters when mounted at the base of the 105mm main armament canon.

F: Merkava Mk III, 188th 'Barak' Armored Bde., Northern Israel, August 1990

In the opinion of many independent military observers, including those from the former Soviet Union and even those who had seen the M1 Abrams in the Gulf War, the Merkava Mk III was an almighty tank designed with pragmatic vision. While resembling its two predecessors in striking fashion, the differences between them and the Mk III were considerable, none more obvious than the modular-type armour applied throughout the tank. The Mk III follows the basic 'Chariot' design and has the same battle-field accessories as its predecessors. These include the 120mm main armament gun base, and the turret mount for a .50 machine gun; the gunner and commander-modified FN MAG cupola-mounted 7.62mm light machine guns; the now ubiquitous ball and chain apparatus; and, of course, a rear storage bin for the crew's equipment (though the Mk III has canvas straps to secure their gear), and additional stores. Seen inset is the ceremonial insignia for the 188th Armored Brigade.

G: Merkava Mk III, South Lebanon, 188th 'Barak' Armored Bde., June 1993

The Merkava Mk III's baptism of fire was, like many incidents in Israel's varied military history, against terrorist forces during a large-scale retaliatory operation in southern Lebanon following increased Hizbollah activity along the Israeli border in the summer of 1993. Though it encountered Hizbollah artillery, rockets and RPGs and Saggers, it did not face off against any armoured vehicles – other than Toyotas and other trucks equipped with twin 23mm anti-aircraft guns. Nevertheless, as one Barak Brigade officer said, 'breaking the cherry is breaking the cherry'. In Lebanon, against real Hizbollah targets, the Mk III proved to be a formidable weapon system. The 120mm main armament cannon became the long-range sniper of the Lebanese landscape and few targets within its range, from a fortified bunker to a mountain top Sagger pit, could escape its destructive wrath.

Notes sur les planches en couleur

A Ces deux chars sont peints selon le motif gris-sable "d'usine" qui appartient au 77e bataillon (Courage) de la 7e brigade blindée, la même unité blindée qui repoussa la machine syrienne dans la Vallée des Pleurs durant la guerre de 1973. La version modifiée présentée ci-dessus arbore le drapeau israélien. A côté, on remarque une boucle métallique du corps blindé, le symbole de la 7e brigade pour les cérémonies et en dessous, les insignes du bataillon.

B Ce char est équipé d'une mitraillette FN MAG de 7,62mm de production israélienne et montées sur la tourelle. La présence ou l'absence d'un canon de .50cal. dépendait de la préférence de l'équipage ou de la probabilité d'une attaque par des vaisseaux de guerre anti-chars ennemis. On voit ici la bannière du corps de blindés (verte et noire) et au dessus le badge métallique porté par les membres du corps blindé.

C1 Comme on le voit sur ce Merkava Mk II en action dans l'enfer boueux d'une petite route de Tyre, la mitraillette FN MAG 7.62mm du commandant du char est équipée d'un viseur de nuit AN/PVS-4 de production américaine. A cause de la boue qui tendait à engloutir les premières tentes des campements, les équipages avaient tendance à stocker tout leur paquetage sur le dessus de leur char en espérant qu'il resterait au sec. Notez le blindage supplémentaire et les boulets et chaînes défensifs à l'arrière de la tourelle. **C2** Ce char est équipé du MCRS rattaché à sa carrosserie. Le MCRS fut extrêmement utile durant les missions opérationnelles au Liban dans la guerre post 1985 contre les Hizbollah, lorsque des mines furent utilisées avec beaucoup d'efficacité.

D Comme on le voit ici, la conception du Merkava en fait un véhicule de combat idéal pour ouvrir la voie à l'infanterie de patrouille lorsque des embuscades ATGW arrêteraient la plupart des chars. Les trois canons montés sur la tourelle servent tout autant contre les avions que contre les menaces représentées par l'infanterie, contre lesquelles ils peuvent envoyer d'énormes tirs de calibre .50 et 7.62. Notez l'intérieur spacieux du véhicule et l'accès à la cargaison arrière/à la soute d'infanterie.

E Ce char, qui fait partie du bataillon Hermon, Aleph ou Compagnie A, Seconde section (comme on le voit dans la marque Aleph/2 placée sur le casier de stockage sur la tourelle arrière sur une toile kaki) est présenté tel qu'il serait durant une patrouille ou des manoeuvres sur le plateau de Golan, la zone d'opérations de la 188e brigade, "face à face" avec les Syriens. Le canon de lourd calibre.50, qui est sans doute l'arme la plus efficace de ce type à avoir jamais été produite, s'avéra particulièrement efficace contre les hélicoptères lorsqu'elle était montée à la base du canon principal de 105mm.

F Les différences entre le Mk I, le Mk II et le Mk III étaient frappantes, mais aucune ne l'était autant que le blindage de type modulaire appliqué sur tout le char. Le Merkava Mk III adopte le modèle "Chariot" classique et possède les mêmes accessoires que ses prédécesseurs sur le champ de bataille. Citons la base de canon 120mm et la fixation sur tourelle pour une mitrailleuse de .50, les mitraillettes de 7.62mm FN MAG montées sur la coupole et destinées au canonnier et au commandant et enfin le dispositif de chaînes et boulets maintenant courant. En encadré, les insignes cérémoniels de la 188e brigade blindée.

G Le baptême du feu du Merkhava Mk Iii fut, tout comme beaucoup d'incidents dans l'histoire militaire variée d'Israel, contre des forces terroristes durant une opération de représailles de grande envergure au sud du Liban après l'augmentation de l'activité des Hizbollah au long de la frontière israélienne durant l'été 1993. Au Liban, contre les vraies cibles Hizbollah, le Mk III s'avéra être un système offensif remarquable. Le canon principal 120mm devint le tireur embusqué longue distance du paysage libanais et peu de cibles à sa portée, qu'il s'agisse d'un bunker fortifié à une fosse Sagger au sommet d'une montagne, réussirent à échapper à sa colère destructrice.

Farbtafeln

A Beide Panzer weisen das gräulich-sandfarbene Farbmuster "ab Fabrik" auf un gehören zum 77. "Oz" beziehungsweise "Courage"-Bataillon der 7. Panzerbrigade derselben Panzereinheit, die im Krieg von 1973 im Tal der Tränen das syrisch Ungetüm in die Flucht schlug. Die oben abgebildete, modifizierte Ausführung ist m der israelischen Flagge geschmückt. Daneben sieht man eine Metallspange de Panzerkorps, das Symbol der 7. Brigade bei zeremoniellen Anlässen, und darunte Bataillonsabzeichen.

B Dieser Panzer ist mit einem auf dem Panzerturm montierten FN MAG 7,62mr leichten Maschinengewehr aus israelischer Produktion ausgestattet. (Ob ei Fahrzeug mit einem 0,50 Kaliber schweren Maschinengewehr ausgerüstet war ode nicht, hing normalerweise von der Mannschaft ab oder davon, ob ein Angriff vo feindlichen Panzerabwehrschiffen mit Hubschraubern zu erwarten war.) Ebenfal abgebildet sind das Banner des Panzerkorps (grün und schwarz) und darüber da Abzeichen aus Metall, das die Angehörigen des Panzerkorps trugen.

C1 Wie man bei diesem Merkava Mk II, der sich im schlammigen Gelände eine Tyre-Pfads einen Weg bahnt, sehen kann, ist das FN MAG 7,62mm leicht Maschinengewehr des Panzerführers mit einem AN/PVS-4-Nachtsichtgerät au amerikanischer Produktion ausgerüstet. Aufgrund des Schlamms, der die vordere Zeltlager meist umgab, hatten die Mannschaften die Angewohnheit, ihre Ausrüstun auf dem Dach ihrer Panzer zu verstauen, in der Hoffnung, daß sie dort trocke bliebe. **C2** Dieser Panzer verfügt über das MCRS am Rumpf. Das MCRS erwies sic bei Einsätzen im Libanon im Krieg gegen die Hisbollah nach 1985 als äußers nützlich, da damals Landminen sehr wirkungsvoll eingesetzt wurden.

D Wie man hier sieht, macht der Aufbau des Merkava den Panzer zu eine optimalen Kampffahrzeug, um einen Weg für Infanteriepatrouillen zu bahnen, un zwar besonders in Gelände, wo ATGW-Angriffe die meisten Panzer aufhalte würden. Die drei auf dem Gefechtsturm montierten Geschütze mit ihren massive 0,50 Kaliber und 7,62mm eignen sich für die Flugzeugabwehr genauso gut wie fi die Abwehr von Bedrohungen durch die Infanterie. Man beachte den geräumige Innenraum des Fahrzeugs und den Zugriff zum hinteren Stau /Infanterietransportraum.

E Dieser Panzer des Hermon-Bataillons, Aleph oder A-Kompanie, zweiter Zug (w durch das Zeichen Aleph/2 auf dem Stauraum auf der Rückseite des Gefechtsturm auf einem khakifarbenen Segeltuch ersichtlich) ist so abgebildet, wie er b Patrouillen oder Manövern auf den Golanhöhen aussähe, dem Einsatzgebiet de 188. Brigade "Auge zu Auge" mit den Syrern. Das 0,50 Kaliber schwere Maschinengewehr, die vielleicht effektivste Waffe dieser Art, die je produziert wurd erwies sich als besonders wirksam gegen anfliegende Hubschrauber, wenn es a der Grundplatte der 105mm Hauptkanone montiert wurde.

F Die Unterschiede zwischen dem Mk I, dem Mk II und dem Mk III fielen ins Aug insbesondere die Panzerung im Baukastensystem, die am ganzen Fahrzeug ange bracht wurde. Der Merkava Mk III entspricht dem zugrundeliegende "Chariot"-Muster und verfügt über dasselbe Schlachtfeldzubehör wie sein Vorgänger. Dazu gehören die 120mm Hauptgeschützbasis und di Montiervorrichtung am Gefechtsturm für ein 0,50 Maschinengewehr, die in de Kuppel montierten FN MAG 7,62mm leichten Maschinengewehre, die für de Schützen und den Panzerführer jeweils modifiziert waren, und die inzwische gängige Kugelkettenvorrichtung. Auf dem kleinen Bild ist das zeremoniel Abzeichen für die 188. Panzerbrigade zu sehen.

G Die Feuerprobe für den Merkava Mk III kam wie so viele Vorfälle in der turbulente Militärgeschichte Israels gegen terroristische Verbände bei einem groß angelegte Gegenschlag im südlichen Libanon im Anschluß an gesteigerte Aktivitäten de Hisbollah entlang der israelischen Grenze im Sommer 1993. Im Libanon erwies sic der Mk III gegen echte Hisbollah-Stellungen als furchterregendes Waffensysten Das 120mm Hauptgeschütz entwickelte sich auf libanesischem Gelände zu Heckenschützen mit langer Reichweite, und wenige Ziele in seiner Reichweite seien es befestigte Bunker oder ein Sagger-Graben auf einem Berggipfel - konnte seiner zerstörerischen Wucht entkommen.